89

P9-DIW-916

The Last Dinosaurs

The editors gratefully thank Claudia Berghaus, Diane Gabriel, and the Geology Section of the Milwaukee Public Museum for their enthusiastic cooperation and technical assistance. And a special thanks to Matthew Peterson, second grader at Catholic East Elementary School in Milwaukee, for his invaluable assistance.

Library of Congress Cataloging-in-Publication Data

Burton, Jane.
     The Last Dinosaurs.

     (The New dinosaur library)
     Includes index.
     Summary: Text and photographic illustrations describe the characteristics and habits of several dinosaurs and other prehistoric reptiles that roamed the earth during the Cretaceous Period.
     1. Dinosaurs--Juvenile literature. [1. Dinosaurs. 2. Prehistoric animals] I. Kirk, Steve, ill. II. Dixon, Doug. III. Title. IV. Series.
QE862.D5B86   1987   567.9'1   87-6463
ISBN 1-55532-286-7
ISBN 1-55532-261-1 (lib. bdg.)

This North American edition first published in 1987 by

Gareth Stevens, Inc.
7317 West Green Tree Road Milwaukee, WI 53223, USA

This US edition copyright © 1987. Based on *The Age of Dinosaurs*, by Jane Burton and Dougal Dixon, conceived and produced by Eddison/Sadd Editions, London, and first published in the United Kingdom and Australia by Sphere Books, London, 1984, and in the United States of America, under the title *Time Exposure*, by Beaufort Books, New York, 1984.

Design: Laurie Shock.
Background photography in selected photos: Norman Tomalin, Paul Wakefield, David Houston.
Photo retouching: Kay Robinson.
Line drawings: Laurie Shock and Paul Robinson.
Additional text: MaryLee Knowlton.
Series editors: MaryLee Knowlton & Mark Sachner.

Technical consultant: Diane Gabriel, Assistant Curator of Paleontology, Milwaukee Public Museum.

5 6 7 8 9 9 92 91 90 89 88

The Last Dinosaurs

Photography by
Jane Burton

Text by
Dougal Dixon

Artwork of Photographed Reptiles by
Steve Kirk

Gareth Stevens Publishing
Milwaukee

Hunting
the
Dinosaurs
and Other Prehistoric Animals

The
First
Dinosaurs

The
Jurassic
Dinosaurs

The
Last
Dinosaurs

The Last Dinosaurs

The first reptiles appeared 345 million years ago and gave rise to the dinosaurs. This book is about the last period — one that began 135 million years ago — in the Age of Dinosaurs.

Sixty-five million years ago the dinosaurs died out. No one knows why for sure, but the end seems to have come suddenly. Many scientists believe a comet struck the Earth, stirring up dust that blocked the rays of the sun for months or years. Without sun, plants would die. Animals would die soon after without food. This is one possible explanation for the end of the Age of Dinosaurs. The mystery remains.

CONTENTS

IGUANODON
and
HYPSILOPHODON

Iguanodon is one of the most famous of the dinosaurs. Many *fossil* skeletons, skin *impressions*, and tracks have been found. The tracks show that Iguanodon traveled in herds. Iguanodon was a plant-eater, or *herbivore*. It had a sharp, horn-covered spike for a thumb. The thumb grew as long as 16 inches.

Hypsilophodon was a small, *herbivorous*, *bipedal* dinosaur. Its long, stiff tail may have been used to balance it as it made quick turns. Hypsilophodon had teeth in the sides of its jaw and a sharp, horn-covered beak in front.

IGUANODON (ig-WAH-no-don)

Length: 29 ft (9 m)   Order: Ornithischia

Location: mostly England and northern Europe; also Rumania, Mongolia, North Africa, and North America

HYPSILOPHODON (HIP-sih-LOH-fo-don)

Length: 6 ft (2 m)   Order: Ornithischia

Location: Isle of Wight (England)

These are the skulls of
Iguanodon (1) and
Hypsilophodon (2). The
beak at the front and the
grinding teeth at the back
tell us these dinosaurs
were plant-eaters.

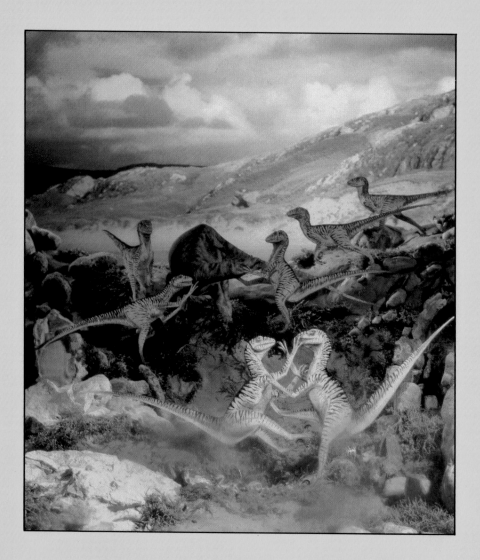

Deinonychus had four toes. One was very small (1). The second carried a huge sickle-shaped claw used in attack (2). The animal walked on just its third and fourth toes.

DEINONYCHUS

Deinonychus was discovered in 1964. It was probably a fast, tough, and fierce bipedal *carnivore*. It was lightly built with long-clawed grasping fingers. When it fought, it probably stood on one foot and used its tail for balance. It would then slash out at its *prey* with its sickle-shaped claw.

Remains of five Deinonychus skeletons have been found surrounding the skeleton of another dinosaur. This is evidence that Deinonychus may have hunted in packs.

DEINONYCHUS (di-NONNI-kus)	
Length: 10 ft (3 m)	
Location: Montana	Order: Saurischia

SPINOSAURUS

Spinosaurus was a huge *carnivorous* dinosaur with a fin, or sail, on its back. The sail was formed by strong spines over 6 ft (1.8 m) tall. These spines grew out of the *vertebrae*.

The sail was covered with skin. It was probably used to control the body temperature. The sail may also have helped other animals recognize Spinosaurus either as an enemy or as a member of its own group.

SPINOSAURUS (SPY-no-SAW-rus)

Length: 39 ft (12 m)

Location: Egypt and Niger   Order: Saurischia

Turned at right angles to
the sun, a sail-backed
dinosaur could *absorb*
heat through the fin.
Facing into the sun, the
dinosaur might *radiate*
heat away from its body.

Quetzalcoatlus (1) was a pterosaur, an animal that could fly or glide. Other pterosaurs were Pteranodon (2), with a wingspan of 23 ft (7 m), and Pterodactylus (3), with a wingspan of 10 inches (25 cm).

QUETZALCOATLUS

Quetzalcoatlus was only discovered in 1971 in Texas. Its wingspan is 39 ft (12 m). This makes it the largest flying animal ever!

Quetzalcoatlus was probably a *scavenger*. Like today's vulture, it would have eaten dead animals. Its body was covered with hair. This hair may have helped it control its temperature. Like vultures, it probably had no hair on its head and neck.

QUETZALCOATLUS (ket-zal-COH-AT-lus)	
Wingspan: 39 ft (12 m)	
Location: Texas	Order: Pterosauria

STRUTHIOMIMUS

Struthiomimus is known as an "ostrich dinosaur." Its back legs were long and slender and built for speed. It had a long neck, a small skull, large eyes, and a toothless beak. It also had three-fingered hands that were just right for grasping prey.

The "ostrich dinosaurs" traveled in herds. They probably had an *omnivorous* diet of insects, small reptiles, and mammals. They may also have eaten fruit, plants, or the eggs of other dinosaurs.

STRUTHIOMIMUS (stroo-thee-o-MI-mus)

Length: 13 feet (4 m)   Height: 6 ft (2 m)

Location: Alberta   Order: Saurischia

Struthiomimus outwardly looked like the large flightless birds of today. Scientists feel that Struthiomimus may have run as fast as today's ostrich — perhaps up to 50 mph (80 kph)!

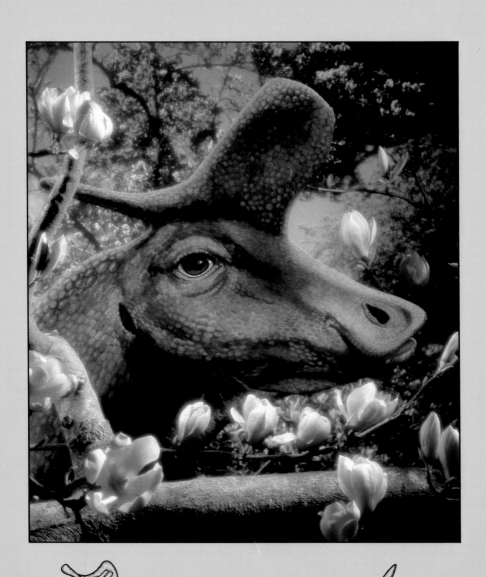

The duck-billed crests of
these dinosaur skulls were
hollow nasal passages that
improved the animals'
sense of smell.

16

LAMBEOSAURUS

Lambeosaurus was a *crested* duck-billed dinosaur. This herbivore had rows of grinding teeth for eating tough plants, twigs, and pine needles. It could store food in its cheek pouches until the food could be chewed.

Lambeosaurus had strong back legs and smaller front limbs. It had hooves on the three toes of each back leg. Two toes on each front limb had hooves, and two had claws. The front hooves have led scientists to believe that Lambeosaurus often walked on all fours.

LAMBEOSAURUS (lam-bee-o-SAW-rus)

Length: 23 ft (7 m)   Order: Ornithischia
Location: Red Deer River (Alberta, Canada)

PALAEOSCINCUS

Palaeoscincus was one of the first dinosaurs to be discovered in the US. This was in the 1850s. Only the teeth were found. Later, part of a skeleton was found. Palaeoscincus was a squat, tank-like animal with heavy armor on its back. Spikes stuck out from its sides.

With this armor, Palaeoscincus was well-protected from the top. Its underside was unprotected. But not many animals could have turned it over to get at it.

PALAEOSCINCUS (pay-lee-o-SINK-us)

Length: 16 ft (5 m)

Location: Montana   Order: Ornithischia

Like Palaeoscincus, Silvisaurus (1) and Scolosaurus (2) were ankylosaurs, dinosaurs with armour or spikes on their backs and tails.

TYRANNOSAURUS

Tyrannosaurus was the largest meat-eating, or carnivorous dinosaur. Thanks to its huge legs, its five-ton body moved quickly over the ground. Tyrannosaurus may have been more of a scavenger than a *predator*. Its teeth grew up to 6 inches (l5 cm) long, and it had a very strong skull. It also had huge neck and jaw muscles. Its strong skull and teeth could have produced enough pressure to crack bones or tear great chunks of flesh.

TYRANNOSAURUS (ty-RAN-o-SAW-rus)

Length: 39 ft (12 m)   Order: Saurischia

Location: Montana and possibly China

Tyrannosaurus could dislocate its jaws like a snake and gulp down great chunks of meat.

PACHYCEPHALOSAURUS

Pachycephalosaurus, or "bone-head," was a bipedal herbivore. It had a keen sense of smell. On top of its head was a thick, bony dome. Pachycephalosaurus probably used its dome for fighting. Like a football helmet, the dome couldn't do much damage, but it could take a lot of battering.

Pachycephalosaurus probably lived in herds. Perhaps head-butting contests took place to see who would lead the herd. These may have been like head-butting contests between mountain sheep of today. When *paleontologists* find Pachycephalosaurus remains, usually only the bony dome is *fossilized*.

PACHYCEPHALOSAURUS
(pack-ee-SEF-ah-lo-SAW-rus)

Length: 16 ft (5 m)   Order: Ornithischia
Location: Montana, Wyoming, and South Dakota

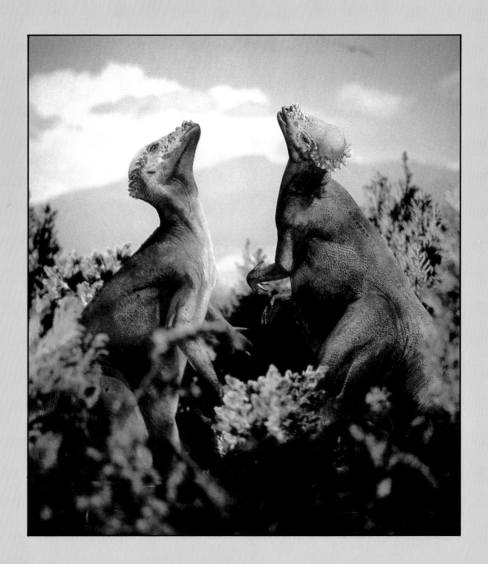

The bony dome of Pachycephalosaurus was up to 10 inches (25 cm) thick and had spikes on the nose and back of the skull.

Fifteen different types of Triceratops skull have been found. Here are four of them: 1) brevicornis, 2) elatus, 3) serratus, and 4) albertiensis.

24

TRICERATOPS

Triceratops is one of the best-known dinosaurs. It was also one of the last. Its head had two eye horns, a nose horn, and a huge *frill* that went over its back. Fossil remains show that it used its head as a weapon.

Triceratops was herbivorous. It nipped off shoots with its hooked beak. Its back teeth worked like scissors. They chopped up food and churned it around inside the cheek pouches.

Triceratops lived on the northern *continents*. As the Earth became cooler, plant life changed. As finding food became harder, Triceratops would become extinct.

TRICERATOPS (try-SARA-tops)	
Length: 36 ft (11 m)	Weight: 8-9 tons
Length of skull: 6 ft (2 m)	Location: Wyoming,
Order: Ornithischia	Colorado, Montana,
	and Saskatchewan

The Red Deer River in Alberta is the
site of many dinosaur findings.
Styracosaurus, Struthiomimus,
and Lambeosaurus are among the
dinosaurs discovered there.

Canada

STYRACOSAURUS

Styracosaurus had unusual decorations on its body. It had a very large skull with a long nose horn and short eye horns. The skull could be as long as one-third the length of the body. Styracosaurus had six large spikes on the back edge of its frill. These spikes probably weren't used in combat. But they must have frightened enemies when Styracosaurus lowered its head. Styracosaurus nipped off plants with a turtle-like beak, and it chopped them up with huge slicing cheek teeth.

STYRACOSAURUS (sty-RACK-o-SAW-rus)

Length: 17 ft (5 m)   Order: Ornithischia

Location: Red Deer River (Alberta, Canada)

Fun Facts About Dinosaurs

1. Here are some animals that appeared at the time of the last dinosaurs and still exist today:

   > paddlefish — Cretaceous period
   > primitive grebes — late Cretaceous period
   > opossums — late Cretaceous period

2. By the end of the Cretaceous period, the time of the last dinosaurs, most of the continents were close to the positions in which they are today.

3. As far as scientists know now, none of today's animals evolved from the dinosaurs of the Cretaceous period.

4. A Pachycephalosaurus skull could be as thick as 9 inches (23 cm). By comparison, the human skull is around one-fifth of an inch (0.5 cm) thick. This would make the Pachycephalosaurus skull about 45 times as thick as a human skull!

5. Anatosaurus had a toothless bill like a duck's. Where our molars are it had huge rows, or batteries, of more than 2,000 teeth for grinding.

6. Some species of Triceratops had horns above the brow that stuck out 3 ft (1 m).

7. Tyrannosaurus could have swallowed a person whole, if people had existed during the time of Tyrannosaurus!

8. Deinonychus could hold its victim with its hands, stand on one foot and, using its tail as a counterbalance, slash open its victim's underbelly with the sharp sickle-shaped claw on its second toe.

9. Dinosaurs and other prehistoric reptiles are not the only animals to have become extinct. Here are some others: mastodons, mammoths, giant ground sloths, giant beavers, and saber-toothed cats. Today animal protection groups work to save rare and endangered animals. Some endangered species are tree sloths, mountain gorillas, aye-ayes, orangutans, rhinos, tigers, and bison.

10. The animals that we call dinosaurs are actually two subgroups of the group called Archosauria. These two subgroups are Ornithischia, which means "bird-hipped," and Saurischia, which means "lizard-hipped." Both groups include some dinosaurs that walked on two feet and some that walked on four feet. Both groups also include meat-eaters and plant-eaters. The division of dinosaurs into Ornithischia or Saurischia is based on the types of pelvis or hips they have.

11. Both dinosaurs and pterosaurs, which were flying and gliding reptiles, belonged to the group Archosauria. The crocodile of today is also an archosaur.

12. A cold-blooded flesh-eating dinosaur would eat its body weight in food in 60 days. A warm-blooded animal would eat its body weight in six to ten days.

13. In August, 1966, 2,000 fossil dinosaur tracks were discovered in Rocky Hill, Connecticut. Fifteen hundred of them have been reburied for preservation. You can see the remaining 500, which are sheltered by a geodesic dome. The exact type of dinosaur has not yet been identified. It is probably from the early Jurassic period. It is thought to be related to Dilothosaurus, whose remains have been found in Arizona. The fossil site is now called Dinosaur State Park.

More Books About Dinosaurs

Here are some more books about dinosaurs and other animals of their time. If you see any you would like to read, see if your bookstore or library has them.

About Dinosaurs. Morris (Penguin)
The Age of Dinosaurs! Parker (Gareth Stevens)
All New Dinosaurs and Their Friends from the Great Recent Discoveries. Long & Wells (Bellerphon)
Brontosaurus, the Thunder Lizard. Halstead (Western)
Did Comets Kill the Dinosaurs? Asimov (Gareth Stevens)
Digging Up Dinosaurs. Aliki (Harper & Row)
Dinosaurs. Jackson (National Geographic Society)
Dinosaurs and Other Archosaurs. Zallinger (Random House)
Dinosaurs and Their Young. Freedman (Holiday House)
Dinosaur Time. Parish (Starstream Products)
The First Dinosaurs. Burton / Dixon (Gareth Stevens)
How Did We Find Out About Dinosaurs? Asimov (Avon)
How to Draw Dinosaurs. LaPlaca (Troll)

New Words

Here are some new words from *The Last Dinosaurs*. They appear for the first time in the text in *italics*, just as they appear here.

absorb ....pull or suck up into something
bipedal (bi-PED-al)................walking or moving on two feet
carnivorous (car-NIV-er-us)
carnivore (CAR-niv-or)...........meat-eating
continents ....the major land masses of the earth. North and South America are continents.

crested	having a bony ridge or a tuft of hair sticking outward from the head
extinct	died out
fossil (fossilized)	the remains or traces of a plant or animal. Fossils are preserved in sedimentary rock formations. Sedimentary rocks are rocks that are laid down in water.
frill	head shield formed of bones of the skull. Probably used to protect the animal's neck and back from attack from above; to scare enemies; and, on males, to attract females.
herbivore (HER-biv-or) *herbivorous* her-BIV-er-us)	a plant-eating animal
impression(s)	a mark, imprint, or mold made by pressure
omnivorous (om-NIV-er-us)	eating a varied diet of plants, meat, insects, and eggs
paleontologists pay-lee-on-TOL-o-gists)	scientists who study fossils
predator	an animal that kills and eats other animals
prey	an animal that is killed for food by another animal
radiate	to give off or spread out, as a radiator gives off heat
scavenger	an animal that eats the leftovers or carcasses of other animals
vertebrae (VER-teh-bray)...	the bones of the spinal column; plural of *vertebra*

Index and Pronunciation Guide

Note: The use of a capital letter for an animal's name means that it is a specific *type*, or *genus*, of animal—like a Pterodactylus or Triceratops. The use of a lower case, or small, letter means that it is a member of a larger *group* of animals—like ankylosaurs or pterosaurs.